AI for Customer Success: Secret Strategies for a Millionaire Business

A secret guide that reveals what customers want and strategies to build a million-dollar turnover, thanks to AI Artificial intelligence that turns buyers into customers for life

Summary

Premise

In a world where technology evolves at a dizzying pace, Customer Relationship Management (CRM) emerges as a beacon in the chaotic sea of digital marketing. This book is an open window into the future, a journey through the innovations that are redefining the way companies communicate, interact and understand their customers.

Imagine a future where AI is not just a tool in the hands of marketers, but an intelligent companion that anticipates customers' needs and desires before they are even expressed. Where augmented and virtual reality transforms every shopping experience into an immersive adventure, and Big Data becomes the compass to navigate the ocean of information. This is not just a dream: it is the reality that is taking shape before our eyes.

Through the pages of this book, you will discover how Blockchain is providing unexpected transparency and security in the digital world, and how Viral Marketing has evolved beyond traditional boundaries, becoming a powerful tool for creating authentic connections with customers. With a particular focus on the hotel industry, we will explore together innovative strategies and case studies that illustrate the immense potential of these technologies.

This book is not just a guide: it is an invitation to look beyond the horizon, to imagine new possibilities and to take advantage of the opportunities that the digital age offers. It is a must-have resource for anyone who wants to fully understand how CRM and new technologies are shaping the future of marketing and customer management.

Welcome to a fascinating journey to the heart of the digital revolution in CRM. Are you ready to explore the future?

The new marketing formulas

Relationship Marketing

The concept of Relationship Marketing was first formulated by RegisMcKenna[1] in 1992.

Relationship marketing refers to marketing focused on the constant goal of establishing a personal and direct relationship between company and consumer. Thanks to it, the "narcissistic monologue" that has marked the last twenty years of the history of business communication has been weakened in favor of behaviors more oriented towards dialogue and listening.

Relationship marketing involves creating, managing, and strengthening strong relationships with customers. The concept of relationship has expanded to include the development of relationships with all those related to the company that can help it serve customers. Employees and partner companies, for example, would be part of this group. Marketing is increasingly shifting its focus from individual transactions to building value-laden relationships and marketing networks. Relationship marketing is more long-term oriented. The goal is to deliver long-term value to customers, and the measure

---

[1] *McKenna, R., Relationship Marketing: Successful Strategies for the Age of the Customer, Perseus Publishing, 1992*

of success is long-term customer satisfaction. This type of marketing requires teamwork between all business departments and marketing in order to satisfy the customer; it requires the development of relationships at many economic, social, technical and legal levels and creates a high level of customer loyalty.

In the new model proposed by Relationship marketing, the relationship (also in terms of shared passion and mutual motivation) finally comes before consumption.

Relationship marketing derives from the awareness, on the part of many companies, that the relational capital of the company with customers, employees and suppliers has much more value for a company, than even its physical characteristics.

It is clear that companies need to rethink better conditions to establish a real dialogue with the consumer/user and to ensure that this dialogue leads to a successful conclusion.

It is important for them to understand that today there is no longer a "consumption that precedes the relationship", so first we equip ourselves with a product considered useful to strengthen the identity and then we talk about it. This model, which until a few years ago worked with extraordinary mastery, is no longer adequate today.

The contemporary consumer is now accustomed to talking, inquiring, reasoning and understanding if it is really worth buying a product before buying it.

Therefore, the relationship that a company must aim for must be one that puts the customer in a position to feel considered intelligent even before being excited by the possible purchase and must ensure that the consumer perceives the communication of the company in question as a real opportunity and not as a vulgar promotion.

Knowledge as a key factor in selecting customers

The most important aspect of relationship marketing can rightly be considered customer loyalty, to be implemented through multiple formulas. To start any attempt at loyalty and customer relations in general, however, it is necessary to know the customer himself. Knowledge, indeed, can be defined as the keystone of every relationship marketing process. A knowledge that is not passive, forever, but active, which evolves over time hand in hand with the history of the company (of its products and offers) and with the history of the customer.

We can distinguish the development of five different levels of relationship with customers who have purchased a product of the company, for example a conference or a banquet:

1) basic: the company only sells the product;

2) responsive: the company sells the product and encourages the customer to contact the company for any clarification or need;

3) Manager: The company representative calls the customer after a short period of time from making the reservation and asks him a few questions. During and after the event, the seller solicits from the customer any

9

suggestions for improving the product and any specific reasons for dissatisfaction. This information helps the company to constantly improve its offering;

4) dynamic: the seller or other company representative telephones the Customer from time to time to inform of improvements made to the service or to make original suggestions about future events;

5) Collaborative: The company is constantly collaborating with the customer and other customers in order to find out how to: increase the value offered.

What are the marketing tools that a company uses to strengthen the bond with the customer and their satisfaction? You can choose between three different approaches, the first is mainly based on adding economic advantages to the customer relationship. For example, airlines offer frequent flyer programs, hotels provide more comfortable accommodations for regulars, and restaurants provide loyalty programs. Although these rewards programs and other economic incentives develop customer preference, they can easily be imitated by competitors and thus fail to differentiate the company's offering permanently. Loyalty programs often use tiered systems to promote customer preference for a product category. For example, the gold, platinum or silver option, gold and diamond. As you move up a level, the benefits for the customer increase. The second approach involves offering both social and economic benefits. In this case, the staff strives to increase social bonds with customers, learning about individual needs and desires and then characterizing and personalizing their products and services. For example, a salesperson develops a good relationship with his customers. Both of these people have created social bonds with the client; This keeps the customer coming back, but it also means that they will often take their customers with them when they leave the company.

This phenomenon is particularly relevant for travel agencies with regard to counter staff. In fact, general managers should initiate promotional campaigns for their key customers; By doing so, when the employee leaves the job, the customer feels that they are maintaining relationships with key people in the company and are not tied to a particular person. The third approach to developing strong customer relationships is to build structural links, as well as economic and social benefits. For example, airlines have developed booking systems for travel agents; regular customers have special telephone lines reserved for them; Airlines have set up lounges for first-class customers and in some cases send a limousine to wait for them at the airport.

Sheraton[2] has made check-in and check-out processes flexible for the best customers; many hotels use technology to deliver a personalized welcome message on the TV in the customer's room, structural changes are difficult to achieve, but it is even harder for competitors to adapt, creating a generally lasting competitive advantage. Among other things, customer frequency is used to help companies record purchases in order to know the purchasing characteristics of their customers and to be able to classify them (Table 1).

	Top	Professional	Entry
Componente A Caratteristiche	✔	✔	✔
Componente B Caratteristiche	✔	✔	X
Componente C Caratteristiche	✔	X	X
Componente D Caratteristiche	✔	X	X
PREZZO	€ 287,00	€ 197,00	€ 97,00

Table.1 – e.g. customer profile

---

[2] Kotler Philip," Marketing del Turismo"; Bowen John T. e Makens James C., 1996,

Definition of Customer Value and Customer Satisfaction: Value Proposition

Customers who exhibit high profitability and frequency deserve management's attention. Sometimes it is possible to increase the low frequency of customers who are highly profitable. Some of them divide their activities among many different suppliers: if we can make our company, their preferred supplier, we can then turn them into our best customers.

For some of the high-frequency, low-profitability customers, there is a chance to motivate them to purchase by showing them the value of additional purchases. For example, hotels can show business travelers the advantage of a VIP floor accommodation that has a lounge with bar service where they can do their business when customers decide not to go to the office. The VIP lounge also offers a fast breakfast service that saves time for the customer; Guests who recognize the value of these services are willing to pay the additional $20 per room. Customers at the low-frequency, low-profitability end are often deal hunters; They show up when there is a promotion and avoid paying full price at all costs.

It is important to carefully study promotions to ensure that this type of customer does not take advantage of offers. For example, if the hotel is fully booked during a holiday, promotions should be excluded or frozen for the period in question. Knowing your customers helps you develop your relationship with them and strengthen it over time.

Today's businesses face the toughest competition in decades, and things will only get more complicated in the years to come.

To succeed in today's fiercely competitive market, businesses need to adopt a marketing strategy.

The answer lies in facing and meeting needs better than others, succeeding, or simply surviving. You need to be "customer-centered," a value that is higher than your target customers.

Companies need to become experts in customer development and not just product development; they need to be able to develop the market, many companies think that winning customers is a marketing sales skill alone, while successful companies have understood that marketing cannot do everything alone. Even the best marketing department is not able to sell products of little value other than to the customer's needs. The marketing department can only work in enterprises where all departments and employees have joined forces to form a system that can deliver superior value in a competitive way. People don't flock to the 28,000 restaurants around the world just because they like the chain's burgers. Customers are drawn to the McDonald's system[3] and not just "its" powered products. Around the world, McDonald's finely designed system provides a high standard of what the company calls QSCV, or Quality, Service, Cleanliness and Value.

The system consists of many components, both internal and external: McDonald's is only successful to the extent that it forges good relationships with its employees, franchisees, and so on to offer exceptionally high value to the customer.

What is meant by Value Proposition: it indicates the package of products and services that represents a value for a given customer segment.

The question that business owners are asked to answer in this block is: "why should customers choose our product/service?"

---

[3] I The McDonalds Corporation. (Tratto dal Web http ://www.mcdonalds. com/corporate/)

How do you generate a good customer value proposition?

1) The first important thing to keep in mind is that there are different ways to create it, namely:

By innovating – creating new value and giving customers something that wasn't there before (the smartphone is one of many examples of innovation within the telecommunications industry).

By making a product/service accessible: that is, allowing segments of customers who previously could not use a product/service, to use it. (e.g. low-cost flights, such as Ryanair):

- Improving a service.
- Decreasing the price of a product/service.
- By solving a specific problem.
- Using brand/status to convey an identity (Rolex, for example, is synonymous with wealth and taste).
- By improving the design of a product (Apple is the best example: it has created high-design technology products).
- Improving the performance of a product.
- Making products more affordable/easier to use.

- Reducing the risks related to a product/service (theft insurance decreases the risks of buying a car).

These methods allow the company to transfer not only the intrinsic value of the product/service offered but, above all, the <u>intangible values</u> that they carry with them. There is no doubt that Apple's value lies not only in the product itself but in all the advantages that the user experiences from using its devices. In addition, Apple[4] means innovation, beauty, safety and the ability to try before buying: its stores allow customers to have an experience with its products before buying them. Today it is a model that is now widespread and almost taken for granted, but even in this they have been important innovators.

2) The second important point to keep in mind is the needs of our customer segments. The Business Model Canvas offers an almost obligatory path, pushing anyone who wants to create their own business model starting from the reflection on the block concerning the customer

---

[4] *www.businessmodelgeneration.com*

segment. Today, no business can survive if it is detached from the needs of the consumer. For this reason, the Value Proposition section emphasizes the need to transfer to customers not only the single product or service, but rather actual and differentiating VALUE.

Customer Retention

The benefits of relationship marketing come from consistently protecting loyal customers, keeping marketing costs down, decreasing loyal customers' price sensitivity, and their collaborative activities. Marketing cost containment is determined by the lower spend needed to retain a customer compared to the expense to acquire it, as well as the creation of new customers through positive word of mouth from loyal customers.

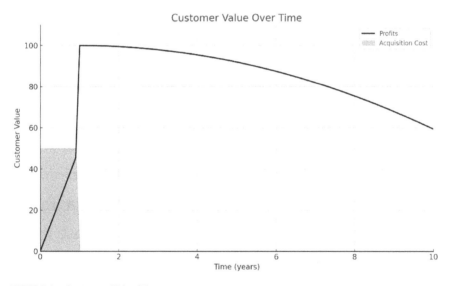

FIGURE 1 - Customer Value/Time

They are less willing to switch to the competition for price and make more purchases than similar customers who are not loyal. Hotel guest collaboration activities include

19

intensive word-of-mouth, business guidance, name giving, advertising, and participation in advisory committees. The combination of these characteristics of loyal customers means that a small increase in customer numbers can produce a large increase in profitability (Figure 1). The researchers found that a 5 percent increase in customer retention increased the profits of nine service groups they surveyed by 25 to 125 percent. As a result, the researchers believe that building a relationship with customers should be a strategic goal of almost every service business. Many products have reached the maturity stage of their life cycle. Competition is fierce and often there is little differentiation between products in the same category. For example, the general managers of the Sheraton in Asia were shown pictures of hotel rooms, belonging either to their own chain or to the properties of three of their competitors. Most directors were unable to indicate the brand name of a room, despite being given a list of eight names to choose from. This exercise explains how difficult it is to distinguish competing hotel brands based on the physical characteristics of a hotel's core product[5].

---

[5] *Kotler et al., 1996; Hospitality, 2000. Harvard Business Review, 1990*

Customer Communication and Management

The word "communication" is subject to countless interpretations and is certainly the most effective and complex tool with which human beings interact and, in order to be part of a community, we can say that it is the only one available to them.

Communication allows us to send signals that, in turn, generate meaningful responses in the environment around us. From this it can be deduced that every human being carries out an exchange with the environment through communication.

Furthermore, we must find the meaning of any communication in the reaction it provokes in the surrounding environment, and discover the message in the reactions it elicits, regardless of the intentions of the person who transmits it. With communication we can deduce both the goal that an individual pursues, and the way of reaction to a given message.

Every behavior is a transformation of internal neurological processes and carries information about these processes. The mini behaviors (eye movements, skin color change, breathing changes) give important information about the person.

Communication can be seen as a feedback system within a "cybernetic system." The response received is the feedback that influences subsequent communication.

"The person acts according to his own internal map, and not according to his own sensory experience."

Each of us perceives the world from the single, privileged point of view of our own frame of reference. As Erickson puts it, "we always translate the other's language into our own."

The world around us is so diverse that we grasp only a few of the many possibilities of interpreting it. And what we grasp is filtered through our individual ways of being, our personal culture, interests, and our past experiences. Each of us lives our own reality, built through the personal use we make of our senses and our impressions of what surrounds us: each of us builds his own model of reality, characterized by individual experience and his own attitude towards the world. The latter is so vast that we need to simplify it, in order to understand its meaning, and we do it in such a subjective way that each of us creates an internal representation that does not necessarily coincide with those of others. The map is therefore not the territory it describes.

Quality of Service

What is Quality? First of all, two types of quality must be distinguished: product characteristics, which increase customer satisfaction, and the absence of defects, which increases customer satisfaction. The first type of quality, product features, is added to the cost of the product: either customers are willing to pay for the additional costs of additional product features, or those features must increase the loyalty of these customers.

For example, hotel rooms on VIP floors offer more amenities than other rooms and charge a higher price. La Quinta Inns & Suites offers free local calls to foster hotel loyalty among business people. Customer expectations are formed through the company's image, word of mouth, the company's promotional offers, and price. The expectations of a customer who pays $45 for a room at Motel 6 will be different from those of a customer who pays $300 for a room at the Four Seasons Hotel in Washington DC. The person staying at Motel 6 may be completely pleased; The features of the room meet his expectations. The first type of quality, the characteristics of the product, are related to the customer's expectations. People who stay at Motel 6 may perceive it as the best quality motel for a price of less than $50; they're not comparing it to a Four Seasons Hotel. Both Motel 6 and Four Seasons Hotel guests will expect the rooms to be hassle-free. For example, the customers of both hotels are likely to become irritated if, when they return in the evening, they discover that the rooms have not been arranged by the attendants.

There is another way to look at quality. A distinction can be made between technical and functional quality. Technical quality refers to what is left to the customer after the conclusion of the customer-employee interaction. For example, the technical quality is related to the guest's room in the hotel, the meal in the restaurant and the car of the rental agency. Functional quality is the process of providing the service or product. While the service is being provided, customers face many interactions with the company's staff. A customer makes a reservation, is greeted by the concierge, is escorted to the front desk by a bellhop, checks in with the receptionist, and is escorted to the room[6].

A hotel's check-in procedure is an example of functional quality; Excellent functional quality can make up for a

---

[6] *Marketing for Hospitality and Tourism (Upper Saddle River, NJ: Prentice Hall). Lambert Carolyn U., Lambert Joseph M. e Cullen Thomas P., 1989, "The Over-booking Question: A Simulation*

room that doesn't quite live up to expectations; If, on the other hand, the functional quality is unsatisfactory, a high-quality room may not be able to erase the customer's previous dissatisfaction. It is difficult to differentiate hotel rooms within the same category. The differentiating factor is not the technical quality, but the functional one. The way in which hotels provide the product (functional quality) or their customer service become the differentiating element. Figure 2 below shows a model of quality of service that uses technical and functional quality as determining factors. Providing quality services and creating value for customers/users is the main imperative.

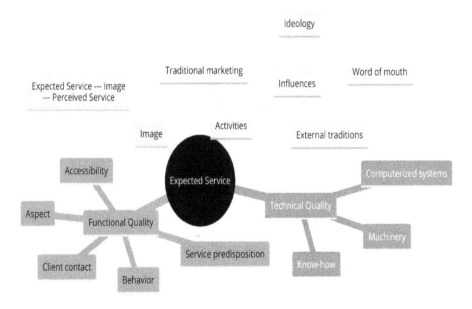

Figure 2 – Quality of Service

Public services, on the other hand, are a clear indicator of a country's state of well-being and characterize its ability to provide: citizens a level of quality of life in step with the best experiences; businesses the opportunity to be globally competitive through the necessary infrastructure and other services.

If by public services we mean those services rendered to the community, expressed by individuals and families, but also by more complex enterprises and organizations, which represent a significant interest to which the State must ensure the adequate availability of quality, it is clear that these services constitute a particularly important object of study, with respect to which it is once again in the interest of the community to be able to ensure coherent management progress with international best practices.

In fact, the inefficiency and backwardness of public services entail serious burdens for citizens and users, burdens that act both directly and indirectly as a weakening of the economy.

In other words, providing quality services and creating value for the customer are not only the prerogatives of private organizations but also the priority goals of public ones. The need of private companies to pursue profit is matched by the need of public administrations to achieve value-generating changes for the country system.

In addition to profit, the positive and correct impact on the environment and on the socio-economic context that private enterprise must achieve must be accompanied by the extensive and pervasive impact of the PA on the entire reference context, including all economic organizations operating on the market.

The concept of quality is a general concept, but applicable to all human realities, what changes is the yardstick of measurement, which depends on two subjects: those who supply the product and those who commission and/or use it.

Hence, the need to identify the subjects and basic elements of the quality of a product/service and the related processes.

For products/services:

1) Who expresses the requirements, needs or needs, usually the Client, and who uses them, usually user, patient, citizen, student;

2) Who provides the product, the service: company, institution, public or private law entity;

The product must have a defined quality, in other words it must be designed and manufactured in accordance with defined specifications and standards and be free of non-conformities or defects.

Factors perceptible by the customer, constitute the main tool for the customer to assess whether what is requested has been obtained, as expected and in a satisfactory manner.

For related processes:

1) The business process must be measurable by means of objective key performance indicators and quality indicators.

2) The monitoring of these indicators over time is a fundamental tool for management to assess the quality and margins for improvement of processes.

Since internal business processes interface with other external processes (of the customer or suppliers), their interface must be defined at the project level.

In addition to technical and functional quality, we believe there is a third element of quality, social (ethical) quality. Ethical quality is a quality based on trust; It cannot be evaluated by the consumer before purchase and it is often impossible to evaluate it after purchase. Some hotel managers don't know the location of fire floors; Other directors know where they are, but they don't train the staff for their implementation. This deficiency in safety management will have no impact on the customer if a fire does not occur. The customer can leave the hotel feeling fully satisfied, ready to return and perhaps recommend it to others. Airlines and hotels that invest in preventative maintenance and train staff for safety purposes usually don't advertise because it's tied to an internal aspect of their products. Businesses need to consider ethical responsibilities when developing products and services, excluding product features that can cause harm and including those that eliminate potential risks. Often these features may not immediately affect customer satisfaction, but in the long run they are able to prevent undesirable situations. Restaurant owners learned this with the bad guys, witnessing the negative publicity that destroyed their businesses, when it was discovered that cases of food poisoning or hepatitis had been contracted in their restaurants.

Social quality connects the design and offering of products that are safe for the customer and society. A business has a responsibility to provide social quality to its audience. It is a valid choice from an ethical point of view and, in the long run, also from an economic one. A widely used model of quality of service is the five gaps model, (Figure 3) which is illustrated in the image at the end of the chapter.

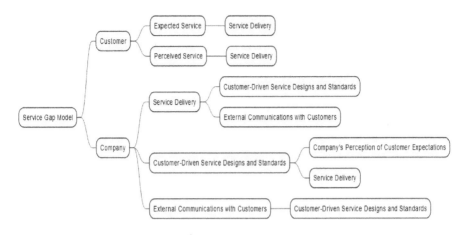

Figure 3 – Gap Model

Measure of perceived quality

To be useful, like any magnitude, the quality of a product, process, service, person, must be able to be measured. In fact, this happens, even if quality assessment is a difficult process, since it is based on a good knowledge of the technical characteristics.

More than thirty-five years ago, Potere Drucker observed with great insight that the first task of a company is to "create a clientele", which can be difficult. Today's customers have a wide array of products and brands, prices and suppliers in front of them, the company must answer a key question: how do customers choose?

The answer is that customers choose the offer that provides them with the most value. Customers are value maximizers, within the confines of research costs and the

31

limits of knowledge, mobility, and income. They form value expectations and behave accordingly; They then compare the actual value they get from consuming the product with the expected value, which influences their degree of satisfaction and purchasing behavior.

Management must remember that consumer expectations vary in favor of their own service expectations and strive to maintain and exceed them.

Luxury hotel customers were asked what hotel features would increase their loyalty to a hotel, and detailed interviews resulted in a list of eighteen possible benefits. Hotel guests were asked to rate each feature on a scale ranging from "loyalty" to "greatly influence" and "loyalty."

In a separate area of the questionnaire, they asked which of these features were offered at the time in the hotels where they were loyal customers.

In this case, you identify the attributes that develop loyalty or value, as well as the areas that most hotels do not offer, giving them the opportunity to create a competitive advantage; Finally, they make it possible to establish the cost of offering these features.

Customer Profile and Loyalty

Tools of the future: "CRM"

The concept of Customer Relationship Management (often abbreviated as CRM) or Customer Relationship Management is related to the concept of customer loyalty.

In a "Market-oriented" company, the market is no longer represented only by the customer but by the surrounding environment, with which the company must establish lasting short and long-term relationships, taking into account the values of the individual/customer, society and the environment. Therefore, attention to the customer is crucial and decisive. For this reason, marketing management must plan and implement specific strategies to manage such an important resource.

CRM[7] basically pushes in four different and separate directions:

✓ Acquiring new customers (or "leads")

---

[7] *https://it.wikipedia.org*

- ✓ Increased relationships with the most important customers (or "cultivable customers")
- ✓ The longest-lasting loyalty of customers who have the greatest relationship with the company (referred to as "prime customers")
- ✓ The transformation of current customers into agents, i.e. consumers who praise the company and encourage others to come to it for their purchases.

Some companies try to ignore customers who are of little importance (defined in jargon as "sub-zero customers") and implement implicit techniques defined, again slang, as "De-marketing".

There are three types of "basic" CRM:

- *Operational* CRM: methodological and technological solutions to automate *business* processes that involve direct contact with the customer.

- *Analytical CRM*: procedures and tools to improve customer knowledge through the extraction of data from the operational CRM, their analysis and the revision study of customer behaviors.

- Collaborative CRM: methodologies and technologies integrated with communication tools (phone, e-mail, App, etc.) to manage contact with the customer.

The most common mistake we make when it comes to Customer Relationship Management is to equate this concept with that of software. CRM is not a simple matter of *marketing* or IT systems, but makes increasingly massive use of IT or automated tools to implement management. CRM is a concept closely linked to strategy, communication, integration between business processes, people and culture, which places the customer at the center of attention in both business-to-business and *business*-to-consumer *cases.*

CRM-related applications are used to keep in touch with customers, enter their information into the *database*, and provide them with ways to interact so that those interactions can be recorded and analyzed.

Before going down the CRM route, every company must be aware that:

You need to invest first in strategy, organization and communication, only then in technology. The choice of software has no effect on the likelihood of success. This does not imply that all software is the same, but it only means that no software will lead to the success of a wrong project.

CRM is suitable for both those companies looking for a fast Return on Investment (ROI) and those that take care of the loyalty process and the increase in the Lifetime Value (LTV) of customers that takes time.

In conclusion, if One-to-One marketing represents the most interesting application of CRM packages and the vast majority believes that it will be a winning weapon to ensure customer satisfaction and (perhaps) loyalty, it is also true that the road to be taken to reach a first phase of its consolidation in the Italian market is still very long. As a result of the rapid changes taking place in the environment in which companies operate, it is now essential for those that aspire to success to pursue the goal of continuous improvement of customer relationships. Customer Relationship Management (CRM) was created to meet this need.

It is, in fact, a strategy aimed at building, developing and maintaining an effective and profitable relationship with customers over time, using all the information that the company can draw about them to increase the level of value proposition perceived by real or potential customers, regardless of the channel of interaction. With

CRM, the focus shifts from taking care of the individual contact to taking care of the relationship with the customer throughout its life cycle; In essence, the profitability of the company is seen as dependent on the purchasing behavior of its customers in the medium to long term. Since the relationships between company and customer tend to develop simultaneously through numerous channels, the complexity of the system increases considerably, bordering on unmanageability. The CRM "system" makes it possible to govern this complexity thanks to a platform of tools with the most advanced solutions in terms of data collection and analysis, content definition, interface, on which the various channels are integrated, allowing anyone who works for the company to have a single view of the customer. At the same time, the latter will be able to choose one of the channels from time to time, for convenience or convenience, always obtaining a service of the same level of quality and completeness.

However, the tools needed to implement CRM, understood as a management approach, transcend the information system alone, although enhanced by the development of information technology. The implementation of a clear Customer Relationship

Management strategy involves a process that involves the entire company. Creating a valid CRM system means, in fact: defining the operational process of operation of the CRM system; adopt a new approach to the market; adapt the company's organizational structure to the new operational marketing logics of the CRM; equip itself with a technical application infrastructure to support the processes defined above. The degree of change required is obvious, but equally evident are the advantages that can be achieved through a CRM process: moving from a redundant and at the same time ineffective management of each customer by the company, by virtue of the different business functions and the different communication channels that interact with it, to a single vision of the customer-company interaction.

CRM Oriented

In today's marketing context, the integration between online and offline experiences is crucial for business success, first of all, it must be kept in mind that there are different tools and different levels of integration when it comes to CRM systems. An excellent CRM system includes a series of infrastructures both at the *front* office level (in the actual external relationship), and at the *back-office* level, to analyze and measure data and the results achieved, but it is equally true that to seek a relationship with your customer you do not always need complicated software. The key is to understand that every touchpoint, whether digital or physical, is part of a single customer journey.

There are many tools available to individual companies in order to establish an individual relationship with the customer, for example:

-*chat online/bot*;

-NFT (non-fungible token)

- Technologies such as augmented reality, beacons, and QR codes;

- *discussion forums*;

- a database (Server, Blockchain) containing the answers to the questions most frequently asked by users (*FAQs*);

- an e-mail address to contact;

- information services also provided on other tools (such as *SMS* to be sent to one's mobile phone, or the use of technology, *APP*);

- on-line ticket for reporting problems or requesting assistance;

- Internal tracking of every communication "from" and "to" the customer;

- Quotes and invoices addressed to the customer;

- History of payments made by the customer;

- Navigation analysis, for profiled users, with the help of web analyzers;

- Social networks; Artificial intelligence.

-Automatic telephone systems that allow many customers to receive the alarm clock simultaneously. Even though the computer wake-up call is impersonal, it ensures that the customer, for example, of large hotels receives his call in a timely and accurate manner.

Businesses that manage to synchronize their online and offline operations can offer services such as in-store pickup of online purchases, improving customer satisfaction and reducing logistics costs.

There are many tools available, and the Internet and the tools it offers can be considered a valid and essential complement to establish and improve the relationship with your customers; It is important to identify which, among many, the company considers to be the best tools for its customers.

From the perspective of companies operating on the Internet, the natural and necessary compendium of knowledge deriving from direct relationships is the knowledge of browsing habits. In this case, the collection of data must be conducted for absolutely internal use and be based exclusively on the routes, times and methods of navigation within the site. Essentially, it is not about collecting information about the user, but about the ways and relationships that the user establishes with the company website. This will allow you to understand which areas of greatest interest and how to optimize your Internet structure, at the service of the customer himself. However, it is crucial to balance the use of data with privacy and security, adhering to ethical and regulatory practices such as GDPR.

In addition, it should not be forgotten that it is not only investments related to technology that are necessary, but above all those in terms of human resources. It is true that information management is being automated, but it is also true that the human component remains a decisive element.

Components of a strategy

The structural components of a CRM strategy are:
Customer relationship analysis and management:
contact with customers and needs analysis through
multiple tools such as mailings, letters, phone calls,
SMS, etc. Contact is essential if you want to map each
individual customer and then organize all the information
collected in a structured database. This information is
valuable as it allows you to know, and, if possible,
anticipate the customer's needs.

The development of personalized content and services:
the data collected are managed for statistical processing
useful for segmenting customers into specific scales.
Once organized, it is possible to proceed with the analysis
of the data to develop a communication and a
commercial and personalized offer.

The IT infrastructure: activation of IT tools that help in
this customer management process.

The spread of information and telematics technologies
has laid the foundations for the development of new
distribution channels, simultaneously intensifying
competition and preparing the ground for new providers
who offer their services based exclusively on Artificial
Intelligence (AI). The majority of banks of significant

size, and also many of the smaller ones, have now activated a futuristic and structural architecture that will open the doors to "WEB3", allowing dispositive operations and no longer just information.

The fundamental element that unites these innovative financial services, which the world's best credit institutions are progressively equipping themselves with, is undoubtedly the centrality of the customer. Putting the customer in a central position in your value proposition is synonymous with the construction and rigorous application of a multi-channel strategy. Obviously, first of all, there is the need to manage the entire range of channels that the banking company intends to use in an integrated way.

The effective integration between the channels is ensured by the preparation of an adequate information system in which all the information relating to the customer converges and is made available to all the channels in order to align their behavior.

An in-depth knowledge of the customer, in fact, allows the bank not only a better understanding of specific needs and a better ability to respond, but the possibility of predicting their desires and offering them "tailor-made" services: in other words, the company can follow behaviors, act in a timely manner and anticipate needs.

The first part highlighted that only 61% of companies have made use of direct marketing and that only a quarter of the latter have invested significantly and only 6% have relevant experience, even if they often resort to external structures.

What are the causes of this unfavorable situation?

The survey suggests the following:

-companies still do not fully understand the importance of the information they already have about their customers, or, rather, they are not able to take advantage of this wealth of information;

-there is a significant lack of creativity on the part of consulting firms, which are still oriented towards "problem solving";

-there is a widespread vision that is too market-oriented and still too little towards the customer, as an individual with specific needs;

-In general, there is a very bad relationship between the quality and price of the supply of goods and services.

The second part of the survey asks what end customers think about it?

29% are defined as "dissatisfied fans", are enthusiastic about one-to-one marketing, but complain about its poor application,

25.7% are the "hostiles", i.e. those who believe in the massification of consumption,

19.5% are "satisfied in favor", sensitive to personalized marketing;

16% are made up of those who are "distant", i.e. unrelated to the issue;

9.8% are "selective in favor", essentially against, but who are in favor of a narrow range of personalized offers.

Technology will become increasingly important with advances in robotics and also helps to involve the customer more and more in service delivery systems.

Artificial Intelligence in CRM - Revolutionizing the Customer Experience

In an era of relentless technological evolution, artificial intelligence (AI) has begun to play a crucial role in reinventing Customer Relationship Management. This chapter explores how AI is transforming CRM, charting a new horizon in relationship marketing.

The introduction of AI in CRM has led to significant automation of customer service. Chatbots and virtual assistants, powered by machine learning algorithms, now effectively handle customer inquiries in real-time. Not only has this reduced wait times for customers, but it has also allowed customer service teams to focus on more complex issues, thereby improving operational efficiency. In a mobile phone company, an AI chatbot, 'Tele-Bot', successfully handles common requests, such as changing tariff plans or checking the balance. TeleBot learns from past interactions, continuously improving its ability to respond in a precise and personalized way. The chatbot handles all customer inquiries initially. Simple requests are solved directly by it, while more complex ones are forwarded to human operators, thus optimizing the workload and improving customer satisfaction.

AI-driven customer service automation is revolutionizing the way businesses interact with their customers. making it more efficient, responsive, and personalized.

AI chatbots have become the first point of contact for many customers seeking support. These systems are able to handle thousands of interactions simultaneously, ensuring immediate responses.

An online bank has implemented an AI chatbot, 'Banker Bot', to answer frequently asked questions, such as balance queries, bill payments, and money transfers. 'Banker Bot' not only handles these requests but is also programmed to detect fraudulent behavior, adding an extra layer of security to customer service. Thanks to machine learning, AI chatbots can now offer more personalized responses. By analyzing historical data from customer interactions, they can adapt their language and tone to mirror the customer's, creating a more human and engaging experience.

A travel company uses a chatbot to provide personalized travel recommendations. Based on the customer's past travel preferences and search history, the chatbot suggests destinations and deals, creating a more intuitive and personalized booking experience for even those most likely to be interested in luxury travel. These customers receive personalized offers for premium travel packages, increasing sales and improving the customer experience. AI can now be integrated with other CRM systems and databases, allowing them to access detailed customer information and provide more accurate and personalized responses.

A retail chain integrated its chatbot with its CRM system and inventory database. When a customer asks about the availability of a product, the chatbot can provide real-time information about availability and suggest alternative or complementary products.

Customer service automation through AI not only improves operational efficiency, but also enriches the customer experience by delivering fast, personalized, and highly responsive interactions, uses sentiment analysis to gauge the tone of customer emails. As technology continues to evolve, AI in customer service will open up new frontiers in customer engagement and relationship management.

AI has revolutionized *predictive analytics* in CRM, allowing businesses to anticipate customer needs and behaviors. Using large amounts of data, AI can identify trends and patterns, predicting future customer needs and thus providing opportunities for targeted and proactive marketing actions.

An e-commerce company uses AI models to analyze customer buying behavior. Based on historical data, AI predicts periods when customers are most likely to make purchases and suggests personalized offers, increasing sales and improving customer retention. It allows for detailed analysis of customer data, providing a deep understanding of their behaviors, preferences, and trends. This includes the analysis of demographic, behavioral, transactional, and web browsing data.

Today, companies, especially those selling electronic products, are using AI to analyze customers' buying patterns, identifying which products are often purchased together. This information allows the company to create targeted promotional packages, increasing cross-selling and customer satisfaction.

Today, large supermarket chains are using AI to predict seasonal variations in demand for certain products. This allows the company to optimize its inventory and promotional strategies, reducing waste and maximizing profits. Enabling more sophisticated and accurate customer segmentation. By analyzing existing data, businesses can create very specific customer segments, allowing for targeted and personalized marketing campaigns. Video streaming companies are already using AI to segment its users based on their favorite genres, viewing habits, and feedback. This allows the company to recommend specific content to each segment, improving customer engagement and loyalty.

Predictive analysis of customer behaviors through artificial intelligence is a crucial element in modern CRM. In an increasingly data-driven market, AI emerges as a key to success in relationship marketing, guiding businesses towards a more connected and responsive future to customer needs, increasingly sophisticated, delivering unprecedented customer experiences

Augmented and Virtual Reality in Experiential Marketing

The adoption of Augmented Reality (AR) and Virtual Reality (VR) is redefining the concept of experiential marketing, creating immersive and engaging experiences that go beyond the traditional boundaries of advertising. This section explores how AR and VR are transforming the way brands interact with their customers.

VR offers a fully immersive experience, transporting customers into a custom-created virtual world. This tool is proving to be particularly effective in experiential marketing, allowing brands to engage customers in unique stories and environments.

A well-known automotive company has launched a VR marketing campaign that allows potential customers to "drive" the new model in spectacular virtual scenarios. Not only does this provide a unique product try-on experience, but it also creates a strong emotional connection with the brand.

AR is changing the shopping landscape, allowing customers to view products in a real-world environment through their devices. This type of interaction provides significant added value, improving the shopping experience and helping customers with their purchasing decisions. A well-known furniture company, on the other hand, has developed an AR App that allows customers to view furniture and decorations in their home before making a purchase. This significantly reduces purchase uncertainty and increases customer satisfaction.

Events and product launches are now enhanced with AR and VR experiences, creating deeper and more memorable engagement. These technologies provide attendees with an unparalleled brand experience that goes beyond simply listening or watching.

A beverage company used VR to create an immersive experience at a music festival, where attendees could enter a themed virtual world tied to the brand, improving engagement and leaving a lasting impression.

A consumer electronics manufacturer uses VR to train retailers on new products. This method allows salespeople to experience the product in a virtual environment, increasing their knowledge and ability to effectively communicate its features to customers.

The use of Augmented and Virtual Reality in experiential marketing opens up new frontiers in the way brands engage and interact with their customers. Not only do these technologies improve the customer experience, but they also provide brands with unique and innovative ways to tell their story, showcase their products, and create lasting connections with their audience. As AR and VR technologies advance, we can expect a future where marketing experiences become increasingly immersive, personalized, and impactful.

Big Data and Blockchain: Personalization, Transparency and Trust

In an increasingly connected world, businesses face the challenge of managing massive amounts of data, keeping up with rapidly changing digital channels and, at the same time, maintaining the security and privacy of customer data. One of the most promising uses of blockchain is in the supply chain, where it can offer unprecedented transparency, from production to consumer. Companies in various industries are using blockchain to track the origin and journey of products, ensuring authenticity and quality. Blockchain can significantly strengthen trust between parties, due to its decentralized and immutable nature. In industries where trust is crucial, such as in real estate transactions or legal services, blockchain offers a means of ensuring the integrity and veracity of information.

Many food companies use blockchain to track the path of its products, from the farm to the supermarket. Not only does this increase consumer confidence in the quality of products, but it also helps to quickly manage any food safety issues.

Modern CRM is powered by big data and advanced analytics, which provide deep insights into customer behaviors and preferences

With the rise of mobile and social media, CRM has evolved to become more dynamic and accessible. Mobile CRM allows businesses and their employees to access important information in real-time, wherever they are, while social media integration provides a direct and effective channel to interact with customers and collect valuable data all within the blockchain. For example, a fashion company can use social media to collect feedback and trends from customers, integrating this information into its mobile CRM. This allows sellers to offer personalized and timely customer service, even on the go.

As businesses reap the benefits of big data and mobile CRM, data security and customer privacy become critical. It's essential to implement robust data security policies and compliance practices to protect sensitive customer information and maintain public trust. Today, almost all banking institutions, using a CRM that integrates sensitive data, adopt advanced security measures such as data encryption and multi-factor authentication, ensuring that customer information is protected from unauthorized access.

Despite its many benefits, blockchain adoption presents challenges, including technological complexity, scalability, and regulatory issues. Additionally, as technology continues to develop, it's crucial to consider the impact on data privacy and security.

Companies adopting blockchain must balance the benefits of transparency with the need to protect sensitive customer information and comply with data privacy regulations.

The convergence of Big Data, mobile CRM, social media, and Blockchain therefore presents challenges inherent in blockchain adoption, ensuring that you reap its benefits while maintaining data security and privacy. A balanced and holistic approach to these elements is crucial to building a robust and secure customer experience in today's digital landscape. Blockchain represents an exciting frontier for improving transparency and trust in numerous industries. With its potential to revolutionize business operations and customer relationships, technology offers unexplored possibilities for a more secure and open future.

From word of mouth to ...... Viral Marketing

The weight of word of mouth in hospitality businesses

High quality creates loyal customers and produces positive word-of-mouth; it is an important factor in the purchase decision; It determines customer satisfaction, which influences the business relationship and word-of-mouth. Studies have shown that the cost of creating a customer is four to six times higher than the cost of retaining an existing customer. Bill Marriott reportedly said that to bring a new customer to a hotel you have to spend $10, but only $10 to make an effort to get him to come back. If a potential customer is satisfied with a hotel, it's hard to convince them to go elsewhere. Often, a substantial price reduction by a competitor will not be enough to push a customer to switch. It's possible that hotel representatives may have to wait for a competing hotel to make a mistake before they can convince a customer to try their services; It could take months or even years. During this time, the salesperson makes phone calls, distributes targeted advertising material and invites the potential customer to have breakfast or a meal at the hotel. The hotel employs financial resources in advertising and public relations and in sending direct mail to the public; It can spend several thousand dollars in an attempt to push a customer to use its products. If an important client decides to use the hotel, the money spent on marketing is well invested. However, if a potential customer tries a hotel and perceives a lower quality of service, they will not return; If this happens, all the marketing efforts made to win over this customer have gone to waste.

A satisfied customer will also spread positive word-of-mouth. On average, a satisfied customer will talk to five others, while a dissatisfied one will talk to ten or more people. In order for the positive word-of-mouth to counterbalance the negative one, it takes at least two customers who leave the hotel feeling satisfied with the service for every person who considers the service to be poor.

A hotel or restaurant that receives mixed reviews is perceived by the market as mediocre; The hotel that strives to develop an excellent reputation must do much better. Accommodations that strive for excellent quality set a maximum number of errors of zero. A 200-room hotel can have more than 50000 customers during the year. Most hoteliers believe that compliance with 90% of the standards is satisfactory.

Every opinion on a hotel or restaurant expressed by relatives or friends has a decisive weight in the choice of a place or a structure. All of us, in fact, feel the need to provide a sort of "service" to those close to us, giving our opinion on the experience we have lived, advising or discouraging it. And our suggestions usually come to fruition.

Word of mouth has, in fact, a very substantial weight on people's decisions: if positive and can become a powerful weapon for winning new customers, if negative a strong deterrent.

This is even more true in the hotel sector: due to the intangible nature of the hotel product, the judgment on it is the means that makes its services concrete.

Word of mouth is a direct marketing tool that, unlike traditional strategies such as advertising and direct mail, is automatically triggered, costs nothing and, if positive, produces incredible effects.

A customer who appreciates the services of the room and the structure, who likes the restaurant menu and who is impressed by the kindness of the staff will remember this experience over time (almost certainly will also want to repeat it) and will not keep his judgment to himself. Every satisfied customer talk about their experience to at least three people. No comment, however, if the stay is "normal", without peaks, because there are no elements to remember. The operator who wants to be on everyone's lips, in positive terms, must differentiate himself from the others, making the stay and the structure special.

Guests should leave the hotel not only satisfied, but amazed, won over by something pleasantly unexpected. A satisfied customer only got what he expected, which is why he is unlikely to talk about it with friends. But if he is impressed by a service or something special, he will share his experience with others. And since customers are not all the same, to amaze them you need to understand their expectations and anticipate them: for some, these are really small attentions.

The customers most attached to the company should be nurtured and pampered because this is what they get the best comments on the structure, but it should certainly not be overlooked those who, precisely because of a positive word of mouth, are on their first stay. A new customer is an opportunity you can't pass up.

The negative customer is dangerous. If there are 3 people reached by positive word of mouth, they become 10 when the judgment expresses dissatisfaction. It doesn't take much to trigger it: a glass that is not perfectly clean at the bar, a stain on the tablecloth, a delay in responding to a request.

Negative word of mouth must therefore be fought and prevented with attentive service, a helpful attitude towards customers, and proper handling of complaints. But be careful: word of mouth is not only triggered by customers, but also by employees who, day after day, experience every detail of the hotel product and talk about it with friends and acquaintances.

Employees are your company's internal customers, they must be followed and listened to so that they carry out their work professionally and efficiently. It is therefore important to create a climate of trust and teamwork, where the staff is involved in decisions and actions and is stimulated to produce the best performance.

Tips: 10 ideas to be remembered

1) Write a thank you letter to the customer after their stay at the hotel.

2) Reward the best customers with coupons for free services (dinner at the restaurant, drinks at the bar, etc.). 3) Send a questionnaire to the children at home to find out their opinion about the hotel.

4) Congratulate customers by telephone on the occasion of their birthday, name day, anniversary or other anniversaries;

5) Send presentation material to customers who ask for information.6) Send, after a month, a photo to the customer taken during his holiday.7) Invite local taxi drivers to dinner. They can be valuable allies for promotion.8) Create a privileged red line for the bookings of the most important customers.

9) Provide all employees with business cards to turn them into hotel ambassadors.

10) Call immediately to thank customers who bring you new and unexpected customers.

A satisfied customer communicates their positive impression to at least three friends and acquaintances.

A "normal" stay does not deserve any comment. There is silence about the experience. The negative opinion of the accommodation facility reaches as many as ten people.

Il Viral Marketing

The concept of viral marketing was also formulated by Seth Godin in 2000, in his book Propagating the Virus Idea, taking up the theory introduced by Malcolm Gladwell in "*The Critical Point*".[8]

Malcolm Gladwell's thesis is that an idea, a fashion, or a social behavior spreads like epidemics. The same mathematical models that explain the spread of the flu or AIDS can help us understand, for example, how people flocked to buy Guru T-shirts or to see the movie Harry Potter, another example: in 1994 a group of a few kids from a small American town brought the Hush Puppies, Classic low-soled suede shoes, from a now bankrupt sale of 30,000 pieces a year to a worldwide sale of 2 million pieces a year simply re-proposing fashion from scratch.

At a certain point, the so-called tipping point is reached, beyond which an avalanche effect is achieved. The

---

[8] Malcolm Gladwell, The Critical Point. The Great Effects of Small Changes, translated by Patrizia Spinato, Rizzoli, 2000, pp. 318

author, in his book, goes so far as to formulate a "law," which he calls the "Rule of 150," which even has the appearance of a scientific law: "It only takes 150 people attending the same five or six bars to cause an epidemic that infects a city of 100,000 inhabitants." Seth Godin takes up Gladwell's theories to formulate a real strategy for marketing.

Bearing in mind that fashions, trends and consequently consumption, often have the appearance of sudden and unstoppable "epidemics", he proposes to investigate which (or rather who) are the so-called connectors, i.e. some subjects (generally few) who propagate the virus which then spreads through "word of mouth".

These connectors can be both leaders of a certain community or group, but also the sellers themselves. Godin, therefore, comes up with a marketing formula that pushes operators in the sector to pay close attention to word of mouth, a very ancient and powerful tool that, thanks to the Internet, has increased its presence and strength.

A viral strategy widely used by large companies is to give away the product you want to advertise to a group of people, so that it circulates from subject to subject, creating a circle of word of mouth that spreads awareness among consumers and triggers their desire to buy it. For example, Sony Ericsson launched its first mobile phone with a camera in the USA, giving it to groups of people who had to be photographed on the street, making the product known and above all making it used, to trigger in the potential buyer at the same time: a new desire, the awareness of a new service and, at the same time, proposing a new game and a way of communicating that was not yet known. Viral marketing, however, is based on an idea-virus that affects everyone it encounters.

There is, therefore, a fundamental difference between "pure" word-of-mouth and an idea-virus: word-of-mouth decreases while the idea-virus grows. The reason is that something or someone amplifies the message to an ever-wider audience. And this is where the network comes into the picture, with a central role (Figure 4).

Figure 4 - Network

Facebook, like any other social network, does not make a message "viral" if it is not born as such. Facebook (social network) can only facilitate its spread, but the seeds of virality must already be present in the idea-virus that you want to spread. It is clear, therefore, that the fundamental difference for the dissemination of the message is not the medium, but the message itself.

The basic idea is that for a viral marketing initiative to be successful on Facebook, the brand must be able to not only tell its story, but also the one that its fans actually want to hear. In practice, we are in a phase of profound change in which an idea can no longer propagate simply by being imposed "from above", but by communicating to the potential user that that idea has an interesting or funny story behind it, and that the user can be lucky enough to share it first.

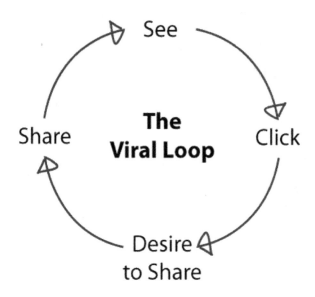

Figure 5 - Viral Loop

In practice, content linked to a particular brand, to be truly viral, does not necessarily have to be linked to a contest or a lottery. Rather, it must convey the user's irrepressible desire to share the content (Figure 5) because that content conveys a message that goes beyond the brand, but enters everyone's personal experience: "I have to share this".

In general, when a brand wants to play it safe, it starts with very trivial initiatives such as lotteries and competitions, the operation of which is already running. But it's the companies that know what they want, that are ready to take risks for something more, that ultimately get the most amazing results. It is clear, however, that the evaluation of the type of customer is the essential starting point for a viral campaign: a very successful musical group can dare, and address a huge audience for its campaigns. A traditional small company, on the other hand, will have to start with small steps and simple things.

Idea/Viral + Means of communication (e.g. social networks) put together and well-structured can become a weapon with immense potential, at any market level.

The three fundamental principles:

1) First Principle of Viral Marketing:

In a given system or process, some people are more important than others.

-Viral Marketing: <u>Grip Factor</u>

Example

The grip factor, a defining element in critical point theory, has enormous implications for the way we view "social epidemics."

We tend to spend our time thinking about how to make our messages more contagious, how to reach as many people as possible with our products and ideas. But the difficult part of communication, however, is to be able to make sure that what is communicated appeals to the emotional memory of our interlocutor, and that it does not enter through one ear and exit through the other.

2) Second Principle of Viral Marketing:

There are relatively simple changes in the presentation and structuring of information that can make a big difference in the impact it can have.

For this reason, high-quality ideas can be much less successful than poor but well-presented ideas.

- Viral Marketing: The Power of Context

Example

In one experiment, two psychoanalysts in New York had a student in a room simulate an epileptic seizure. When there was only one person listening behind the door of the next room, they rushed to the student's aid in 85% of cases. But when the subjects thought there were more than four people who could hear the student, they rushed to help only 31 percent of the time.

3) Third Principle of Viral Marketing:

The power rule of context holds that human beings are much more sensitive to the environment in which they live than we are led to believe.

For this reason, it is necessary to always think about how one's idea can act on a single person and on a set of several people.

The three principles of Viral Marketing help to understand the meaning of the epidemic, first of all by clarifying how it is possible to reach a "tipping point".

Customer Satisfaction and Infidelity
Its strategic value

The use *of customer* satisfaction must be accompanied by an innovative policy direction, it must be considered in a "high" dimension compared to the mere measurement of user satisfaction, so as to be able to give him specific meanings of real challenge to change. Its strategic aspects are summarized below, as they have already been mentioned above in the context of the report. In the more general field of evaluation, the role of statistics is certainly aimed at the production of statistical indicators of the context and of the activities carried out, of the services obtained.

The survey of *customer satisfaction* must generate a virtuous process between measurement and actions to improve the service and therefore in this sense it takes on the meaning of a useful tool for the continuous improvement of the quality of services.

Customer satisfaction measures the satisfaction of their expectations if customers have gotten what they expected, they are satisfied; If their expectations have been exceeded, they are extremely satisfied Customer, on the other hand, measures how likely they are that customers will return and are willing to do collaborative work with the organization.

Through the search for satisfaction with the service provided, a profound transformation of relations between institutions, citizens and businesses must take place, based on the reciprocal ability to listen, so as to ensure that the public administration acquires the *trust* of the citizen. The issue of user satisfaction in the Public Administration therefore assumes a leverage meaning to build a new model of administration/administered relationship based on trust and a new legitimacy of public action.

In addition, each user of a service interprets his satisfaction in the light of two completely personal elements: expectations and perceptions: the former influenced by individual aspects and also by communications through "word of mouth" and past experience, the latter influenced by the information that has been provided by the manufacturer - public administration.

Expectations and perceptions can also change over time. The problem for a flexible P.A./Company *is* not only to find a score that measures the value of satisfaction, but above all to be in a position to know how to follow the changes in users' expectations, to continuously adapt its internal processes and the behaviors of its professional resources.

Infidelity Customer

Is customer satisfaction a requirement of loyalty?

Customer expectations must be met or exceeded to foster customer loyalty. However, satisfied customers may not become loyal customers for several reasons. First, some travelers do not visit the same area on a regular basis; So, a customer may think that a hotel is beautiful, but never returns because he no longer goes to that location. Second, some customers like to try different hotels and restaurants when they return to an area; They may be happy with each hotel or restaurant, but they keep giving back to add new experiences. Third, some customers are price-sensitive and will choose the cheapest offer; Even if they were satisfied with the last hotel, they will try another one for the new offer received. Finally, customers expect to remain satisfied with the purchases they make; otherwise, they would have given up. As a result, the ratings tend to be overly positive. To develop customer loyalty, managers must provide maximum satisfaction. Two researchers found out why 90% of customers who switch providers were satisfied with their previous provider. In addition, Heskett, Sasser and Schlesinger, [9]developers of the service profit chain model, found that the link between customer satisfaction and loyalty was the weakest of those within their model. So even though customer satisfaction is a requirement of customer loyalty, that doesn't mean they'll come back. The important point of this discussion about satisfaction and loyalty is that loyal customers are worth more than satisfied

---

[9]*The Service Profit Chain (New York: Free Press). "Hotel Values Profit from Service", 2000*

customers, a customer who does not return and does not express a favorable judgment about the company.

The equation "satisfied customer equals loyal customer" - with all that this entails, such as lower management costs for call centers - does not always correspond to reality. Customer "satisfaction" expresses an attitude, while "loyalty" refers to customer behavior.

In some areas of demand (e.g. cars), 40% to 70% of customers who say they are satisfied do not actually remain loyal to the brand.

According to the methodology suggested by Garh Hallberg[10] and called "Differential Marketing", it is preferable to identify a group of customers that is able to ensure a significant part of the turnover and focus marketing actions on this group to try to consolidate their link with the company.

It is necessary to act above all on the customers who produce the most important margins, involving them with targeted information actions and taking into account that a large part of the target may be made up of excellent customers of the competition.

---

[10] *The Differential Marketing Strategy for Brand Loyalty and Profits, Garth Hallberg.*

For example, the real trend of the recession has been an increase in 'infidelity' accompanied by a rejection of luxury products as well. It is this more promiscuous and less loyal clientele, that of luxury brands, that have had to innovate to attract new customers again.

This type of clientele must be involved, but it must be considered that inadequate promotional actions can shift the focus from quality to price.

Consumers are thus formed by judgments about the value of sales offers and make their purchasing decisions in accordance with them.

The satisfaction of the customer in relation to a purchase depends on the performance of the product in relation to a buyer's expectations. The levels of satisfaction that a customer can experience are varied: if the performance of the product is below expectations, the customer remains dissatisfied; On the other hand, if it is superior, the customer remains very satisfied or enthusiastic.

Expectations are based on the customer's previous shopping experiences, the opinions of friends and colleagues, as well as information and promises from market participants and competitors. Operators need to be careful to set the right level of expectations: if they set expectations too low, they may satisfy buyers but fail to attract enough buyers; Conversely, if expectations are raised too high, buyers are likely to be disappointed. They aim high because they know that customers who are only satisfied will continue to easily turn to other suppliers when presented with a better offer.

There are countless tools to assess customer satisfaction and systems based on complaints and suggestions: a customer-centric organization makes it easier for customers to provide suggestions and make complaints. Although the customer-centric company tries to offer a high level of satisfaction compared to the competition, it does not aim to maximize it.

Marketing Focus describes how companies measure customer satisfaction.

For customer-centric businesses, satisfaction is both a goal and an important factor in business success. These and other companies understand that highly satisfied customers bring several benefits to the firm: they are less price-sensitive and remain customers for longer periods (Figure 9); Over time, they make additional purchases when the company introduces related products or improvements, and they speak favorably to others about the company and its products. In order to ensure consumer loyalty, brands must work hard to ensure a strong, more unprejudiced relationship with a consumer/customer. "Individuality" and "Communication" are the key, in order to convince the consumer that the product will be shaped specifically to their needs. The relationship with the customer is maintained by informing him, since too often it is precisely the information - from that on the products - that is lacking.

It is therefore necessary to reiterate their 'singularity' in any sector, even in the luxury sector. If this marketing

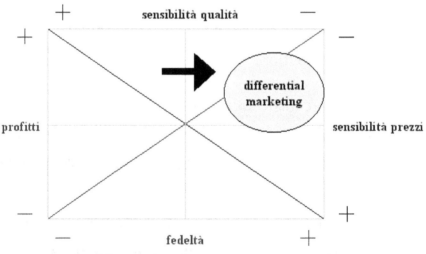

Figure 6 – differential marketing

communication strategy[11] is established, a relatively small group of customers is able to guarantee a high volume of sales and, more importantly, a good operating margin.

Only in this way do the company's marketing choices prove to be truly successful, since a close correlation is created between loyalty and profits, a relationship that can further develop over time.

Resolving customer complaints

According to Michael Shepard, general manager of the Savoy Hotel in London, "Customers are less forgiving. The competition allows them to expect a flawless offer without any tolerance for mistakes.

 If something goes wrong and is fixed, the customer may come back, but if the problem is not resolved, they will not come back at all."

Resolving customer complaints is a critical component of customer remediation. A study by the Technical Research

---

Considerations taken from "The Interactive Strategies of the Enterprise" by Richard Normann and Rafael Ramirez

Programs Institute found that 11-91% of customers who file major complaints will never return, while if the issue is resolved quickly, 82% will return; The resolution of complaints therefore brings down the percentage of customer defections from 91% to 18%. By resolving minor complaints, it can go as low as 5%. There are two important factors in resolving complaints: firstly, the resolution must be swift - the longer it takes, the higher the defection rate will be - and, secondly, customer complaints must be uncovered.

The convention organizer booked a bus to take a group of club managers on a visit to a sports club; The bus was scheduled to depart at 9:30 a.m. on Saturday morning; The bus company usually scheduled the arrival of the bus at least 15 minutes in advance of the departure time. The organizer began to worry when, at 9:20 a.m., the bus had not yet arrived; He called the employee of the transport company who told him in a detached way that the drivers were still sleeping and would not arrive at the scene until 11 a.m. because they had apparently been engaged in an excursion that had not ended until 2.30 a.m. the previous night and federal regulations impose a minimum interval of eight hours between one trip and another.   The organizer requested a fleet of taxis to transport his group so they wouldn't miss the 10 a.m. appointment and then called back to cancel the bus. On Monday, he phoned the bus company to obtain a refund of the full amount requested in advance at the time of booking; The right to a refund was denied for lack of at least 24 hours' notice from the termination. After several weeks of phone calls and a letter, the company agreed to reimburse the sum paid; Six months later, the organizer received an additional check for $125 and a letter of apology from the national sales director. The bus company reimbursed the cost of renting the transportation and added $125 but still lost the customer.

After six months, the organizer had found another company and was satisfied with the service; He had no intention of changing. If the bus company had promptly refunded the sum and offered a $125 rebate on his next trip, perhaps they would have been able to keep the customer. Discerning leading companies jump on complaints because they know that every customer communicates three things:

- You can still win my trust if you show that you personally care about me and solve the problem. It is not certain that our business relationship and my word of mouth will have to stop. And even though I'm threatening to leave, if I didn't really care I would have done it without needing to tell you;

• I represent other people. Realize that if I'm not satisfied, neither are others. You should be really grateful to me for that, because the quieter customers who are just as dissatisfied have quietly abandoned you or will do so at the first opportunity;

• I'm pointing out to you the negative results produced by the flaws in your systems and your business philosophy. Think of me as a fire alarm. I'm warning you that something bad is about to happen that requires immediate attention. So, whatever you're doing, you'll want to change quickly. Another critical aspect of complaint resolution is that most customers don't complain. They do not give the possibility of solving problems; they just leave and never come back. Managers need to develop systems to encourage customers to complain. Methods of hunting for complaints include helpline numbers that encourage customers to report problems they encounter. Scorecards encourage customers to discuss issues with the product.

Managers need to train staff to pay attention to customers who don't seem satisfied and attempt to understand their problems. Another way of collecting complaints is through a service guarantee: in order to invoke the warranty, they must complain. When a customer complaint, business managers should be grateful. As Janelle Barlow and [12] Claus Moller write in A Complaint Is a Gift: "When customers feel dissatisfied with products and services, they have two options: they can say something or leave." If they leave, they essentially give no chance to the organizations to remedy their discontent.

Customers who complain have not yet stopped the dialogue and offer the opportunity to return to a state of satisfaction that makes it more likely that they will make a new purchase. So, as much as we may not like negative feedback, customers who complain are giving us a gift. If we shift our perspective in this direction and see complaints as gifts, we can more easily use the information produced by complaints to grow our business.

---

[12] *Hospitality: Berlow e Moller, (2000).*

Complaining customers are one of the most available and yet most underutilized sources of customer and market information. Letters of complaint should be dealt with quickly by post or telephone. If you respond by letter, it is a good idea to partially personalize the letter, showing that you know the customer's specific complaint and what will be done to prevent it from happening again; You have to offer the customer a solution to the complaint.

A more effective way to resolve the complaint could be through the use of the phone;

It is often less expensive to make a phone call than to send a letter; The phone call allows for personal contact with the customer and allows the manager to analyze the details, finding out exactly what happened to the customer. The worst thing a company can do is send a formal letter that shows no understanding for the customer's problem or no response at all.

Bob Martin, a former professor at the University of Nevada in Las Vegas, was spending the summer season working as an administrative assistant at a vacation resort. One day he was in the general manager's office when he began to complain about a pile of letters from dissatisfied customers to which he had to respond. The manager then stated that he hated having to respond to complaint letters and also hinted that it was a waste of time because he would be lucky if only 5% of them returned to the hotel.

Bob picked up the pile of letters and said, "I'll take care of it." As he left, he added, "I'll bring them all back." Bob Martiri wrote a letter thanking customers for the time they had taken to write. He apologized for the problem and cited the initiatives taken by the hotel to solve the problem.

He offered customers a complimentary stay and asked them to call the executive secretary to complete the reservation; This made them feel important and in the tourist complex to identify returning customers.

The author closed the letter by expressing the hope that the initiatives following the complaints would not be exploited only by other people and that the recipients of the letter would become valuable customers again. By the end of the summer, 90% of the authors of the complaint letters had returned or made reservations for a future date; The lifetime value of these customers exceeded $100,000.00 in revenue. The resolution of complaints also transformed the much negative publicity through word of mouth into positive publicity; Some of the returning customers had in fact convinced other couples to follow them.

Complaint resolution is one of the easiest ways to plug the hole in a "leaky bucket"; It's an effective way to prevent customer defection: managers should look for complaints and resolve them quickly.

Cost of lost customers

Businesses need to pay close attention to their customer churn rate and take steps to reduce it. First, the company needs to define and measure its churn rate; Then, it needs to identify the causes of customer churn and determine which ones can be reduced or eliminated. There's not much you can do for customers leaving the region or business travelers leaving the business; However, there is a lot you can do for customers who leave because of poor service, low-quality food, or excessively high prices.

The company needs to have a frequency distribution analysis that shows the percentage breakdown of customers who churn for a variety of reasons. Businesses can calculate the profits lost in the event of excessive customer churn; For each individual customer, this value is equivalent to that of their life cycle. Ritz-Carlton understands that the total lifecycle value of its regular customers is more than $100,000.00; This value is calculated by measuring the average annual purchase of an individual belonging to that market segment and multiplying this value by the average lifespan of a member of that segment. The average lifespan is established through surveys or through customer registration. People move, they are transferred, they change companies and they become dissatisfied; So, the average lifespan of a single business traveler could be as high as four years. Hotel chains that have a customer registration system in place can track the overall value of a customer for the entire chain and not just for a single hotel. The life cycle varies by location and market segment; It's unique to each individual company.

The company needs to calculate the cost of a decrease in churn rate: if the cost is less than the amount of lost profits, it is right to use that sum to reduce the churn rate. Today, the best companies go to great lengths to retain their customers. Many markets have reached maturity and the number of new customers is limited in almost all categories; Competition is increasing, and the costs of attracting new customers are rising.

In these markets, attracting a new customer could cost five times more than keeping a satisfied customer. Offensive marketing normally costs more than defensive marketing, as it requires a lot of effort and spending to snatch satisfied customers away from the competition.

As a result, even if current strategies focus heavily on marketing mixes that aim to create sales and new customers, the company's first line of defense lies in customer retention. The best way to retain customers is to offer them high satisfaction, which translates into high loyalty.

- A study carried out by a French call center company Vocalcom Satmetrix, highlights the most common causes of customer disloyalty. Around 12 million French customers were surveyed who switched suppliers (in essential sectors) in the last six months after a bad customer experience. The three most common causes of customer infidelity are pricing, unjustified additional costs, poorly handled customer service. Precisely because of this service, the infidelity rate has dropped by almost 40%. Customers who left their supplier were four times higher than average.

These examples show us how customers stopped buying the product, reduced its use, or turned to a new supplier. It is necessary to constantly monitor the "customer defection rate" (lost customers/total customers), which is inversely proportional to the level of satisfaction.

The survey of lost customers has a high rate of return on investment because it allows you to accurately identify competitive disadvantages and areas of dissatisfaction in a short time.

Lost consumers can often prove to be a valuable source of information about the mistakes made by the company and possible solutions.

What strategies to adopt:

o Define the characteristics of a lost customer (how long it has been since they have purchased, how long they have turned to competitors, etc.);

o define who is responsible for identifying lost consumers; structure a database with lost customer names; structure a questionnaire to analyze in detail the reasons for defection;

o use telephone interviews;

o present yourself to the customer in a correct and courteous manner;

- briefly justify the investigation (example: "We noticed that you have not purchased our product for X time and we would like to know what influenced your decision");
- make it clear that the interview will not last long;
- accept a possible refusal without trying to force the interviewee to respond;
- if the consumer buys from a competitor, ask what characteristics prompted him to change;
- understand the customer's purchasing criteria and process;
- define who has played the role of decision-maker in the purchasing process;
- Investigations can be done by an external company or by a neutral internal employee.

Tips:

- Interviewers need to be able to guess if it is possible to retrieve the customer and decide how to behave;
- The more time that passes before you get back in touch with your lost customer, the less likely you are to get them back.
- the data must be readily available and easily available;

- data on lost consumers must be analyzed through group analysis and reported on control sheets, such as a Pareto chart, on which the characteristics offered by the competition can also be reported;
- losses must be quantified in terms of lost market share and unrealized profit;
- Analyze the list of lost consumers and check if they have common characteristics (income, age, gender, etc.) in order to have a complete picture of the areas of dissatisfaction[13].

- "Brand loyalty and less and less dissatisfied customers", this must be the new motto in the world of Marketing.

Robert Salvoni, Satmetrix International Managing Director, says "...I can't understand why so many companies still haven't figured out what the customer's needs are" ... "I'm perplexed that *brands* still don't listen to or underestimate what customers are saying."

Big brands tend to raise prices and increase the number of paid services, this will help the growth of customer "volatility". The study conducted by this company also shows that companies do not help teams understand the

_____

implications of their behavior on customers. Given the current economic situation and the strain applied to every level of sales and profit margins, it seems unacceptable to lose customers for reasons that are totally within the company's control. It seems that companies are not able to fully understand the benefits of valued and acquired customer service. When a "brand" communicates to one of its customers the promotion in progress, it generates a higher loyalty rate and positive word of mouth, avoiding possible abandonment and therefore at the same time decreasing the potential negative trend. Robert Salvoni concludes that: "the study demonstrates the doubled positive effect, generated precisely by the acquisition of new satisfied customers for a brand".

The "case" of a customer, Elisabetta and the life insurance policy: ..." she seemed satisfied with the response she received in the branch, ... instead?"

A customer, Elisabetta, goes to her bank to take out a life insurance policy. On the instructions of a bank employee, he tells Gianni, a member of the bank's staff, about his wish. Gianni listens to her but, given the particularity of the request, he directs it to Mario, a colleague of his who is a specialist in the field. Mario, as soon as he finishes talking to his boss, receives the customer in a pleasant living room and she tells her again about her need.

In the end, Mario presents her with two excellent alternatives. When she has finished listening, Elisabetta thanks her and leaves. The next day, Elisabeth receives an online questionnaire with the classic question: "How satisfied are you with your last visit to our branch, between 1 and 10?" Elisabetta thinks that she has obtained a valid advice but also the commitment she had to make ... He thinks for a moment, then replies 8. The following week, however, Elizabeth took out her policy at another bank.

The bank's managers, happy with the flattering vote, did not activate any initiative to improve the experience of the next Elisabetta and not lose her as a customer. But if Elizabeth had been able to recount her experience, she would have expressed herself more or less like this:

"I wanted to take out a life insurance policy, so I went to my bank for advice. At the bank, an employee told me to contact Gianni, to whom I explained what I wanted. Gianni, however, redirected me to Mario, the specialist in the life sector. I waited for Mario to finish talking to the director, and then I had to tell for the second time what I wanted. In the end, Mario seemed competent and gave me interesting advice."

Already with this feedback, the bank could have taken action in five directions:

1. Act on the culture, making its employees aware of the fact that customers always take precedence over any internal task.

2. Activate a system to share customer appreciation and criticism in real time with employees.

3. Intervene on training to increase the technical readiness of front-line employees.

4. Review the branch's processes and organization to define more effective ways to direct customers to the employees who are best able to meet their needs.

5. Activate a feed-back to the customer of the actions taken following their reports to strengthen the relationship.

In practice, the bank could have reduced the turnover rate of customers, increased cross-selling and, at the same time, increased its purchasing capacity[14].

The story of Elisabetta's experience explains how, investing through new technologies such as "Text and

---

[14] Source: Newsstand

Sentiment Analysis" is now possible to collect, analyze and disseminate Customer Voice (VoC) in real time, permeating the entire organization with the culture of customer experience excellence. The customer experience has become, in fact, the main factor that distinguishes companies on the market and translates into being able to provide the right product to the specific segment in the time and manner expected by customers. Customer Voice (VoC) is a cognitive tool that reveals trends, intercepts emerging problems, changes in needs, desires and feelings, in the light of which to develop new opportunities, solve problems before they create damage, optimize skills and processes so that the network can provide products and services that meet customer expectations.

Given the growing development of new ways of contact, an effective Real Time Customer Voice Program involves the analysis of the different touch points that mark the bank/customer relationship, as well as new modes of expression including social media (in particular Facebook), whose rapid evolution is a wake-up call for banks of the importance assumed by these communication channels.

Rediscovering open-ended questions, given the amount of information potentially available, the best way to start and consequently suggested is to "rediscover", within the existing VoC Programs, the classic open-ended questions. Comments provided by customers often provide insights and answers to questions that sometimes companies had not even asked. For example, in a recent survey conducted according to "classic" methods in which the client was made to experiment with the use of the Text and Sentiment Analysis technique, it was discovered that:

• In addition to the numerous factors proposed, among the reasons for choosing the bank, the real reasons lay in aspects that can be traced back to the concept of ethics that that organization transmitted... an aspect completely neglected by management;

• it was possible to identify alternative ways of segmenting customers in relation to the "desired profiles" to which to direct appropriate service models that better met specific needs;

• what were the most satisfied and loyal types of customers related to the service models offered;

• How best to serve profitable customers.

The maximization of the potential provided by this type of data (unstructured) is obtained by reading integrated with the data already typically held by the company (structured). For example, specific aspects of the customer experience such as the difficulty in completing a certain online transaction can be read in relation to demographic aspects (e.g. man, 45-60 years old).

Another fundamental aspect is the need for Real Time Customer Voice Programs to become an essential aspect of organizational culture capable of pervading processes, decisions and actions and the culture of all the resources involved.

In this regard, effective Real Time Customer Voice Programs provide that the information collected from customers is made available through structured Customer Feedback Management systems. Another fundamental aspect for the success of a Real Time Customer Voice Program is represented by the bank's Customer Orientation culture. Also, for these needs, the use of Text and Sentiment Analysis techniques for listening to the voice of employees can be a very rich source of ideas for collecting suggestions and information on what the front-line is able to grasp from customers, as well as factors capable of keeping their motivation high.

The *"Nespresso" case*

Nespresso is a famous brand of coffee; it has been in our homes for many months now but many consumers still cannot understand how the company has managed to infect so many consumers in such a short time.

But what does this have to do with marketing and sales? In a period of full economic recession, it is one of the few shops with a queue at the entrance... Is that enough for you as an observation? The secret of their success: selling "coffee and emotions". The purchase is experienced as a real guided experience through a visual path of elegance and luxury, the pod becomes an object of desire equal to an object of the highest goldsmithing.

Why build all this around a pack of pods for a few euros? The customer does not buy the pod, the customer buys the exclusive *"service"* and the luxury treatment reserved for him, the customer knows that by buying a simple coffee machine he can be projected into a muffled world for a few minutes.

Every detail seems to be aimed at this purpose: the affiliation of customers takes place through a registration and the possession of the free card that allows you to enter the prestigious Nespresso Club, thanks to which you have the opportunity to be always updated on the brand's news and exclusive initiatives.

Even the furnishings of the stores, well-kept and avant-garde, convey that sense of exclusivity typical of a high-level sports club; After purchasing, the consumer is also invited to taste a coffee from the line completely free of charge at the mini bar of the same store. The same goes for the employees' clothing, in addition to being coffee shades, it is taken care of to express composure and professionalism.

We could hypothesize three main reasons that have directed the brand to make a choice of this type and reach a large slice of the market: the first is a repositioning of the target, Nespresso in fact has been able to intercept what remained of a market now considered vintage or that of espresso coffee machines to be used at home and with a technological innovation and a glamorous positioning has literally reopened a market, it also sees among the major Nespresso buyers a new slice of young people ranging from 25 to 30 years old, previously absent.

The second is the need for a massive, very solid endorsement with Clooney, rather than Damon. Third, but not least, is the excellent strategy of affiliation and customer loyalty with an improvement in the quality of the (intangible) perceived service.

In short, the Nespresso customer is not a consumer as such but a consumer as part of the Nespresso family as if he were an employee. Truly an excellent marketing operation. Nespresso.... "What else?"[15]tag.

---

[15] http://www.nestle-nespresso.com/about-us/our-history

Conclusions

Most of the weaknesses considered above can be traced back to strategic management that underestimates the importance of the customer and focuses too much on cost containment. In addition, as is often the case with many companies, almost disregarding the management of those already acquired. Another critical point on which the company should invest more is the development of a monitoring of the internal environment (resources, skills, communication) and the external one (suppliers, market, customers, competitors) which would increase the effectiveness and decision-making autonomy of a company.

In summary, it is precisely from a more accurate management of the customer portfolio that the company should start working. By knowing the customer better, you can better identify their needs and satisfy them more confidently and easily, thus reducing the level of customer defection. In the previous pages, the crucial importance of a customer-focused orientation and a quality management system capable of minimizing possible quality drops and promptly recovering from situations that have gotten out of hand has been widely emphasized.

If we then consider that the initial prerequisite for the creation of a relationship of stable and mutual profit must necessarily take into account full customer satisfaction. Once this obstacle has been overcome, the next step would be to get to know the customer with whom there are points of contact. Based on a better knowledge of each customer, the company could customize its offer according to the principles and potential of CRM. Although the path to the creation of a Customer Relationship Management system is anything but simple, the internal structure of the company and the external environment have the necessary characteristics to be able to effectively start it. First of all, to improve the transition relationship with the main customers, through the deployment of investments and resources, aimed at the most profitable ones. As we have seen, in fact, the company currently has great difficulty in identifying, and subsequently, satisfying, the most important customers.

It is necessary to measure the degree of customer satisfaction with appropriate tools such as Customer Satisfaction, investing in a targeted manner on those from whom a greater economic return is expected, on the company side and on the greater service offered/perceived, on the P.A. side. The ultimate goal of this strategy, as reported in the chapters, is the creation of mutually beneficial relationships, determined not only by complete satisfaction, but by the development of trust, and therefore, of "loyalty", on the part of the customer.

Dear reader,

I hope you found "AI for Customer Success" engaging and thought-provoking. Your opinion is incredibly valuable to me, not just to understand what I've done well, but also to help me improve my future works.

If you enjoyed the read, I would be immensely grateful if you could take a moment to leave a review on Amazon. Reviews help other readers discover new books they might love and provide essential feedback that helps me grow as an author.

It doesn't have to be long or complex – even a few words are enough. Just share your thoughts to help spread the word.

Thank you for your support and for spending your time with my story. It's because of readers like you that I can continue to write and improve.

With gratitude,

Leo Foster

Bibliography

Anolli L., *Fundamentals of Communication Psychology*, Il Mulino, 2006. - Arielli E., Scotto G., *Conflicts and mediation*, Milan, Bruno Mondadori 2003- Crosby, "Quality means compliance with requirements." 1979 Winners Cullen Thomas P., 1989, "The Over-booking Question: A Simulation -Fornell, C. *The Satisfied Customer. Winner and losers in the battle for buyer preference.* Palgrave Nacmillan 2007. Hospitality: Berlow e Moller, (2000) Malcolm Gladwell, *The Critical Point. The Great Effects of Small Changes,* translated by Patrizia Spinato, Rizzoli, 2000, pp. 318. Lovelock, 1992; Murdick et al., 1990.

McKenna, R., *Relationship Marketing: Successful Strategies for the Age of the Customer,* Perseus Publishing, 1992

Pacori M., *The Secrets of Communication,* (last edition) 2007, Milan, DVE Editore. Italian Review of Evaluation, 26: 113-123, 2003.

Considerations taken from "The Interactive Strategies of the Enterprise" by Richard Normann and Rafael Ramirez - Etas Libri. "All Consumers are not created equal" by Garh Hallberg - Publisher John Wiley & Sons. - Rumiati R., Lotto L., *Introduction to the psychology of communication,* Il Mulino, 2007.

Sandhu et al. (1991, 1993). -The Service Profit Chain (New York: Free Press). "Hotel Values Profit from Service", 2000,

Kotler Philip," Marketing del Turismo"; Bowen John T. e Makens James C., 1996, - Kotler et al., 1996; Hospitality, 2000. Harvard Business Review, 1990

Upper Saddle River, NJ: Prentice Hall "Marketing for Hospitality and Tourism" Lambert Carolyn U., Lambert Joseph M. - Urbani G. *An evaluative experience in the public administration: the People Satisfaction project.*

Susie Linder-Pelz. *NLP Coaching: An Evidence-Based Approach for Coaches, Leaders and Individuals.* Kogan Page Publishers, 2010. pp. 22

K. ISHIKAWA, *Guide to quality control, Industrial engineering and technology,* Asian Productivity Organization, Tokyo. 1976, Joual of Remi Bankirig, 1993-1994